GW00832971

Verses From Hampshire

Edited By Allie Jones

First published in Great Britain in 2018 by:

 Young**Writers**

Young Writers
Remus House
Coltsfoot Drive
Peterborough
PE2 9BF
Telephone: 01733 890066
Website: www.youngwriters.co.uk

FOREWORD

Welcome, Reader, to *Rhymecraft -
Verses From Hampshire.*

Among these pages you will find a whole host of poetic
gems, built from the ground up by some wonderful young
minds. Included are a variety of poetic styles, from
amazing acrostics to creative cinquains, from dazzling
diamantes to fascinating free verse.

Here at Young Writers our objective has always been to
help children discover the joys of poetry and creative
writing. Few things are more encouraging for the aspiring
writer than seeing their own work in print. We are proud
that our anthologies are able to give young authors this
unique sense of confidence and pride in their abilities as
well as letting their poetry reach new audiences.

The editing process was a tough but rewarding one that
allowed us to gain an insight into the blooming creativity
of today's primary school pupils. I hope you find as much
enjoyment and inspiration in the following poetry as I
have, so much so that you pick up a pen and get writing!

Allie Jones

CONTENTS

Thomas Withers (8)	71
Phoebe May Smith (8)	72
Jasmine Stone (7)	73
Jessica Lewis (7)	74
Holly Jones-Cassidy (7)	75
Jayden Ruff (8)	76
Lily Adams (8)	77
Olivia Keen (7)	78
Lara Hooper (9)	79
Nancy Rose Smith (7)	80
Isobel Macaulay (7)	81
Owen Piner (8)	82
Luke Williams (7)	83
Leigha Lisa Davis (9)	84
Ben Brett (9)	85
Evie Speight (8)	86
Jacob Jay Taulbut (8)	87
Kiera Fryer (7)	88
Kieran Yinhu Richardson (7)	89
Logan James Hall (10)	90

New Milton Junior School, New Milton

Ali Bunnett (9)	91
Molly James-Croft (10)	92
Maddie Hendy (10)	94
Sammy Lillington (9)	96
Weronika Ewa Marciniak (8)	97
Alice Green (7)	98
Martha Westaway (9)	99
Elif Stamcheva (7)	100
Allana Hendry (8)	101
Romilly Lewis (9)	102
Katie Gazzard (9)	103
Reanna Rarela (8)	104
Alissa Carroll (8)	105
Ruby Jenner (9)	106
Eva Costello (7)	107
Charles Peacock (9)	108
Olivia Elizabeth McCracken (7)	109
Emma Rebbecca Hall (9)	110
Ellen Hiscott (9)	111
Ryker Augustine (8)	112

Harvey Brown (8)	113
Charlie Michael Hooper (8)	114
Lily Mays (10)	115
Megan Guppy (7)	116
Maisie Wardle (8)	117
Mia Bibin (8)	118
Lydia Buswell (8)	119

Preston Candover Primary School, Preston Candover

Ffion Turberfield (10)	120
Izzy Richardson (10)	122
Evie James (10)	125
Thomas Gray (10)	126
Mimi Jones (10)	128
Jane Lang-Horgan (10)	130
Charlotte Gent (10)	132
Ollie Webb (10)	134
Harry Jones (9)	137
Tom Loftus (9)	138
Oliver Whittle (9)	140
Evie Mattia (10)	142
Libby Joanne Crosswell (9)	144
Leo Bradley Lewis Jackson (9)	146
Isabella Bevilacqua (10)	148
Monty Leonard-Wright (11)	150
Charlie Jones (9)	152
Adam Pugh (9)	154
Erin Lawson (10)	156
Harry Edward Christopher Seaman (10)	157
Oliver Coplestone (9)	158
Nina Acedańska (8)	159
Harry Jason Corney (8)	160
Oscar Mattia (8)	161
Willow Pajaree Fannon-Vickery (8)	162
Lorna Turberfield (8)	163
Raphael Martin-Reynolds (8)	164
Edward William Corney (8)	165
Noah Taylor (9)	166
Evie Loftus (8)	167
Connie Leonard-Wright (9)	168

THE POEMS

My Disney Tale

As I wake in the early hours, my stomach flutters with extremely excited butterflies.
The excitement of travelling to the place of dreams where wishes come true.
As we arrive at the iron gates of sparkling, special dreams,
I see the tall and tremendous Cinderella's Castle.
The tower points and sparkles in the sun like crystals shining on a princess' tiara.
It is so high it nearly touches the sky.
In the near distance you can see mouse-shaped ears of excited families enjoying the magic.
We walk through the main parades,
the sound of music and Disney characters dancing along to every clear beat, makes me start tapping my feet, with a need to join in. Evening fireworks light up the sky like an exploding volcano, all pretty colours of the rainbow in all shapes and sizes.
Snap, *crackle* and *pop* and many more noises makes me jump out of my skin.
Cinderella's Castle looks like a complete fairy tale and I have found mine.

Eve Cordelia Mansfield (9)
Alverstoke CE Junior School, Alverstoke

Animals In The Seasons!

Spring, spring, wonderful spring
Baby lambs are born
Bunnies leap out of the burrows to eat
The emerald-green, shiny and new grass.

Now it's summertime, the flowers are blooming
And it is starting to get hot
The children are splashing by the rock pool
They see a crab scuttling along the steaming sand
to cool off in the rock pool.

Now it's autumn it's starting to rain
The leaves are changing from green to purple,
orange and brown
Try to catch them as the wind blows them to the
ground
The wolves in the woods start to go hunting in the
moonlight and howl at the midnight moon.

Now it's winter it's getting colder and darker
It's starting to snow and hedgehogs are
hibernating

All cosy and warm tucked up tight
Till spring arrives.

Elizabeth Panter (8)

Alverstoke CE Junior School, Alverstoke

Dream

I saw the flowers on the window,
And it was a pretty day,
But you were hiding behind the curtains,
You were slipping away!

The sun was shining,
The sky was bright,
The trees were hiding,
Into the night...

The dark was coming,
The wind was blowing,
The birds were dancing,
Their wings were glowing!

The clouds were talking,
For these beautiful girls,
The moon was walking,
Spreading stars as pearls, pearls, pearls...

I saw the flowers on the window,
And it was a pretty day

But you were hiding behind the curtains,
You were slipping away!

Kristina (Krisi) Dayan Georgieva (8)
Alverstoke CE Junior School, Alverstoke

All About Me And My Friends

Me and my friends having fun,
We will always be in the sun.

Me and my friends love to swim,
We love to go to the park to swing.

Me and my friends love to go sailing on a boat,
If it rains we will wear our coats.

Me and my friends love to dance,
Especially when we get the chance.

Me and my friends love our bows,
We always line them up in rows.

Me and my friends love our art,
We are all very smart.

My mum always likes to bake,
So me and my friends will eat the cake.

After school we love to rest,
All my friends are the best!

Lauren Brown (8)
Alverstoke CE Junior School, Alverstoke

Animals' Dreams

Animals around the world dream at different times.

The snake ate the cake while he took a break at the lake.

The toucan drove a car to a bar with her ma.

The mouse was as big as a chair.

A rhino had a horn as sharp as a knife, so does his wife.

The tamarin couldn't see a beautiful tree.

A flying lizard could fly like a fly.

The tapir surfed on the lake but he fell into the lake but he was a good swimmer.

The jaguar watched a TV in a tree.

A bushbaby grew some crops on a farm.

The eagle flew an aeroplane from Asia, South Africa and South America.

The sloth rode a bike in the big city on the road going too fast and he crashed.

Finley McQuillan (7)
Alverstoke CE Junior School, Alverstoke

Aeroplane

4 o'clock, time to go,
We will be in a taxi that's on the road,
In the airport, breakfast time,
Then we hear the plane landing, bell chime,
Oh no, I spoke too soon!
We will be waiting all afternoon.
Put your suitcase in the machine,
And my bladder is full with wee,
In the toilet when I flushed,
It sounds like my head's been crushed.
Our plane is finally here,
And I can see it in the clear,
Seen our suitcases on the trolley,
And I'm feeling rather jolly.
Day and night we are finally here,
And Dad peeks at a can of beer.
What will happen on...
Our way back!

Lily Anise Francis (7)
Alverstoke CE Junior School, Alverstoke

Untitled

Let's give a round of applause for the star that twinkles,
Star and twinkle.

I give them vegetables in the morning,
And most of the time I'm always yawning.

My guinea pigs love to squeak,
But most of the time the go *weeecck, weeecck*.

They run around in their hutch,
And they eat their breakfast in a cup.

We cover them over at night,
And when it's morning, we let them out to enjoy the morning light.

They whizz around in their tunnel,
We give them a lot of grass, actually let's call it a bundle.

Lily Crosley (7)
Alverstoke CE Junior School, Alverstoke

Lick A Lot

Have you met my new puppy?
He is cute and fluffy here
and there like a teddy bear.
His tail wags at 100 miles per hour
Like a speed boat propeller at full power.
His nose is wet and cold
like an ice cube in a mould.

P ounces around, crazily,
U p and down the garden path,
P anting extraordinarily fast,
P atting him on the head when he brings the ball
  back,
Y aps all the time as if to say, 'Mummy, Daddy!'

And his name is Lickalot!
He does, you know!
Lick a lot.
Lick a lot.
Lick a lot.
I love Lickalot.

Sophie Weston (7)
Alverstoke CE Junior School, Alverstoke

Speed Of Lightning

F antastic Lewis Hamilton takes the win again.

O con and Perez crash once again in Belgium.

R omain Grosjean gets an eight pointer in a badly performing car.

M ercedes have an outstanding pole position for the 70th time.

U mbrellas shield the drivers from the sun and the rain.

L ights shining in Singapore as they race round the track.

A t last, only one lap to go.

O ne car, one winner, one race.

N ew drivers always need to practise.

E veryone cheers when the winning driver's front wheels go over the line.

Benjamin Davis (8)
Alverstoke CE Junior School, Alverstoke

Animal Dreams

Farmer Joe is saying goodnight,
To all the animals snuggled up tight.
Connor the cow and Harry the horse,
Are dreaming that they're on the animal course.

Charlie the chicken and Peter the pig,
Are dreaming that they're wearing a funky wig.
Still in the hay, all snuggled up tight,
The animals dream of things that are bright

But then comes the time, everyone's horror-struck,
In comes an Enderman and everyone screams like
a guitar pluck.
He steals the blocks and everyone's cold,
But they stole back the blocks and that's another
story to be told!

Eden Millie Gransden (9)
Alverstoke CE Junior School, Alverstoke

About Minecraft

M inecraft is the best because YouTubers play it.

I love Minecraft because it is as great as school.

N o fools are allowed to play fun Minecraft because they might break the electronics and then there would be no more Minecraft.

E xciting new things to do on Minecraft every day.

C rafting houses and killing enemies.

R eading how to play then being an expert.

A dventures in the dark forest as dark as night.

F un things you could do on amazing Minecraft.

T o be an expert you need to read the instructions and play it every day.

Elise Koh (7)

Alverstoke CE Junior School, Alverstoke

Four Seasons

A new year starts
It brings four season
Each one different
For many reasons.

Around the time of March
I hear the birds sing
For sure I know
It's the beginning of spring.

Now it's June
The weather is warmer
There's no school for weeks
It must be the summer.

Now it's September
It brings a late blossom
Lots of nice colours
It's definitely autumn.

Short days and rain
It's so cold it's bitter

I wish it was spring
I'm fed up with winter!

Nicolas Dunning (7)
Alverstoke CE Junior School, Alverstoke

Football

F ootball, football, how I love football! Playing with friends, play with Dad!

O ut about in the stadium, lovely to watch!

O ff down the wing I go, going full flow, whizzing past defenders, crossing and scoring.

T rying to score, trying to win every match, we play as a team.

B ertrand, Southampton's ace, tackling, winning balls, running down the line.

A tlético Madrid winning La Liga lots and lots.

L oving football, never not loving football lots and lots.

L acazette scoring every week, every game!

Rudy Harbour (7)

Alverstoke CE Junior School, Alverstoke

The Underworld

Underneath the rock,
You'll find bedrock.

Bedrock, the invincible rock,
Indestructible, black and grey.

Finding red stone, finding iron,
Finding coal and diamonds.

Portals leading to other lands,
Like Happy, Nether or the End.

In Nether, meet and defeat,
Zombies, Withers and Ghasts.

Venture into Happy Land,
Or meet me at the end.

A dragon waits for you to stay,
And purple-eyed Endermen stare.

Underneath the rock,
You'll find Bedrock.

Joseph St John (7)
Alverstoke CE Junior School, Alverstoke

Cara, My Sister

C ara is an amazing artist.

A nd she is smart which is how she got into this poem.

R eally missing her, now we're alone.

A mazingly happy for her, wish she had a clone.

M ystogan is a character she draws.

Y ou are the best sister ever.

S o I could ask for no better.

I ntelligent beyond measure.

S till we really miss her.

T raumatising to not see her.

E nding this poem is hard for me.

R eaching my sister, this was for you, you'll see.

Hugh Hutcheson (8)

Alverstoke CE Junior School, Alverstoke

Minecraft - Mining, Crafting, Farming

Go out at night and you'll get a fright.
The Enderman's head fills me with dread.
Blown up by a creeper?
You'll be meeting the Grim Reaper.
The spider bit him on the head,
And now the poor player's dead.
When on a cliff edge always crouch,
Because if you fall, you'll get an ouch.
Never give a llama a hit,
You'll end up covered in slobbery spit.
Take a sheep and do some shearing,
Snip, snip, snip, you'll be hearing.
I think Minecraft's totally fab,
Playing every day is never drab.

Dylan Murchie (7)
Alverstoke CE Junior School, Alverstoke

I Love My Family And Friends

I love my magical mum,
She's lovely and always laughs with me when something funny happens.
I love my doodling dad,
He's so spicy and loves any hot spices or chillies.
Kind Kai is very kind,
But he is not only a little bit cheeky but he is really cheeky.
Caring Chris is always nice to me
And is never, ever a snitch.
Naughty Nacho is very scratchy and loves to bite.
I love my friends and family, they're the best,
I love them very much!
Will I be a mum one day?
I would love my kids.

Mae Ryan (8)
Alverstoke CE Junior School, Alverstoke

Minecraft

You have to be fair when you always dare,
You see green and black sparkling things,
Oh, danger, danger, it's a creeper!
Let's go, run, run!

There are purple jewels when you fall,
You might build a wall or nothing at all,
You definitely don't want to go wrong.

Spiders have red, gloomy eyes,
If you bump into one, prepare to be surprised,
These nocturnal creatures prowling the night,
Lurking around to give you a fright.

Minecraft, unleash your imagination.

Archie Hills (8)
Alverstoke CE Junior School, Alverstoke

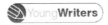

Rhymecraft

Iron door, iron door, please don't lock,
I will mine through the night so I can stock.

Diamonds, emeralds, gold and more,
Coal, bricks and iron ore.

Llamas, cows, sheep and a pig,
Steve and Alex want to dig.

Skeleton, zombie and Enderman,
Don't look into their eyes or they'll kill you again.

Adventure, survival or create,
In the end, it's always late.

Pickaxes, swords, fist and bow,
I'll fight them until the final blow.

Jonathan Geary (8)
Alverstoke CE Junior School, Alverstoke

Lego

I have lots of Lego, it is so much fun,
But tidying up is a pain in the bum.
When I wake up in the morning all I want to do is
play,
But pesky school stops me being Cole every day.

Buying Lego is my favourite treat,
But my daddy doesn't think so when he hurts his
feet.
Fireman in Lego City or a knight,
Lego city police officers chasing criminals in the
night.

I really do like Lego, playing the games and
building things,
I really like the stories that my Lego brings.

Ruari Flanagan (7)
Alverstoke CE Junior School, Alverstoke

The Steps To Becoming Decapitated In Minecraft

Oh look, a creeper over there!
I've had them come and give me a scare.
I'm looking for creatures big and small,
The Enderman, the one that's tall.
I'm mining for diamonds in the dark,
As I hear a loud bark!
I'm building a house that's very tall,
Then I see another player building a wall.
I'm in the Nether mining Nethercrack,
Not knowing there's a blaze behind my back.
I'm in the end not thinking I'll be dead,
And then I end up losing my head.

Caleb Dyer (10)
Alverstoke CE Junior School, Alverstoke

I Love Pugs

I love pugs because I love when they look grumpy and they're so cute.

L ittle pugs I love more, but I still like big pugs.

O ccasionally I even dream about pugs.

V ets make poorly pugs better.

E very time I see a pug, it makes me happy.

P ugs have been my favourite since I was about six and a half.

U nder the table I see a cute sleeping pug.

G ummy bears I like, but I like pugs more.

S o, do you like my sentences about pugs?

Charlotte Scott (7)
Alverstoke CE Junior School, Alverstoke

Dinosaur

D einonychus would slash its prey with its sharp claws

I chthyosaurus did not lay eggs like any other reptiles

N igersaurus had a spiky, long neck

O rnithopods had a hard head to charge at things and smash them

S uchomimus was a huge, strong dinosaur that lived by rivers

A llosaurus is nine metres long and allosaurus means 'a different lizard'

U rbacodon had a frill on its tail

R ugops was a scavenger and didn't attack other dinosaurs.

Elijah Adams (7)
Alverstoke CE Junior School, Alverstoke

Going To The Nether

I'm mining in darkness and I can see nothingness.
I finally found lava, now I'd rather get water.
I've got water.
Oh no, I'll need to slaughter!
I got my obsidian, a creeper went oblivion!
I'm making my portal and there's loads of mortals.
I'm in the Nether, I won't live forever.
I see a blaze then I run into a maze.
I see a ghost but my luck won't last!
I need a plan but I see a wise man.
I buy a potion, I need a good motion.
I say bye then I die!

Asher Dyer (9)
Alverstoke CE Junior School, Alverstoke

All About Cooking

I like cooking, we all like cooking
But there's one thing that we like the most about
cooking: eating!

Baking, making, icing are all fun
But the tasting is what I like most about baking.

Washing, washing, all about the washing
This is the least thing I like about baking.

Oven, oven, all about the oven
But when it goes in the oven, I am as bored as a
penguin sitting on the egg.

Food, food, all about the food
What will I do without you?

Hermione Goldby (7)
Alverstoke CE Junior School, Alverstoke

Minecraft!

M ining in the darkest night, giving me the biggest fright!

I tried to make a farm for food.

N ow's the time, time to kill zombie pigmen.

E ver tried to kill an Enderman? Nah, too scary!

C raft a diamond sword, stick, diamond and... diamond.

R un as fast as you can! Creepers coming to kill, they're up the hill.

A t the hill creepers are happy to kill.

F ight to the death in Minecraft realm!

T ime to say bye and hello to the void!

Zoe Walker (8)

Alverstoke CE Junior School, Alverstoke

Lego Ninjago

The ninjas protect the city of Ninjago,
They swing their weapons high and low.

Garmadon is a baddie with four arms,
He fights with weapons and he has no charm.

The master of energy is Lloyd his son,
When he's not fighting, he has a lot of fun.

The master of ice is Zane,
He is a robot but still feels pain.

Kai is the master of fire,
He is good but is a liar.

Samukai is made of bones,
And he always moans.

Matthew Scott (7)
Alverstoke CE Junior School, Alverstoke

Emojis

Emojis are happy and sad
Some are really, really mad
Emojis are the best
They never rest.

Share your laughs and cries
Or send one with really big eyes
Send a girl in class a kiss
Oh, don't read that, Miss.

My best emoji is the love heart
And there's even one for when you fart
Pass on a clap or high-five
To let them know I'm alive.

With one emoji it can show your mood
And a picture could show your favourite food.

Olly Ray Riggs (7)
Alverstoke CE Junior School, Alverstoke

Panda

Look at Panda on the wall,
She thinks she's the best cat of them all.
She climbs the trees and bites the leaves,
A funnier cat you won't believe!

She plays in my garden
And hunts out spiders.
Then argues with birds
Before climbing in houses.

I play in the street which Panda observes from a
roof up above,
Where she can pounce and swerve.
As I go down the street fast on my bike,
She runs after me quickly, the little tike!

Chara (8)
Alverstoke CE Junior School, Alverstoke

Minecraft Monsters

M y favourite monster in Minecraft is a Wither,

I t eats anything in its way,

N o time to lose, get to protection,

E nter the pirate ship I built in the bay,

C reepers are green monsters full of TNT,

R un away and get clear from the blast,

A fter you escape, hunt for a portal,

F lee to the Nether where you might see a ghost,

T ake a second to switch to creative and make
your player an immortal.

Arnie Benjamin Gransden (7)

Alverstoke CE Junior School, Alverstoke

Shiny Diamonds

I have now found a mine,
But there are still things I need to find.
I am now stuck in a hole,
This is a problem I can't solve.
Terrors could be right there,
But also there is very fresh air.
I can't stand on four legs in the morning,
But I can stand on two in the afternoon,
Shout and they'll come after you.
Get ready for a bad night,
As you're in for a fright.
I may not seem too bad,
But inside I am very mad.

Florence Elizabeth Hind (8)

Alverstoke CE Junior School, Alverstoke

Rhymecraft

R oofs, windows, walls and doors,

H ouses, bricks, wooden floors,

Y ou can build a roller coaster to go round and round,

M e, I build them then knock them down,

E veryone who likes Minecraft,

C ould play all night,

R emember that creepers can give you a fright,

A fter you've finished saving the day,

F ind the box and put it away,

T hanks for listening to my rhyme.

Charlie Ward (7)
Alverstoke CE Junior School, Alverstoke

Halloween

In the deep, dark night,
When the moon was bright,
I saw a pumpkin light,
Trick or treat?
I want to get some sweets,
As I run away from the werewolf,
With his big, hairy feet,
Because I don't want to be a piece of meat,
So I hide in the woods,
With Little Red Riding Hood,
In the dark, dark night,
We see the small lights,
It has the werewolf,
Our eyes were like a prize,
Just like that, we were dead.

Joe Maniatis (8)
Alverstoke CE Junior School, Alverstoke

Minecraft

M ine at day, not the immoral night.

 I s Minecraft always bright?

N ice monsters? There are none!

E vil Herobrine always completes his tasks.

C rafting is so easy, just follow the recipe!

R un! Or else the creepers are gonna explode!

A n angry Enderman can always give a fright.

F arm animals, hmmm, I only need wheat and seeds.

T ry to mine at night, not a single diamond.

Liam Walker (8)

Alverstoke CE Junior School, Alverstoke

How Minecraft Works

M inecraft is the best of all games.

I nside is a world of Heaven.

N ever doubt Minecraft.

E specially escapist in Minecraft.

C reativity is the most popular part.

R eliable, Minecraft is.

A fter 2005 they were billionaires.

F ound in the world of Minecraft is Happy Land.

T ruly the minds of Minecrafters are wonderful. Minecraft is the best!

Oliver John Janes (10)

Alverstoke CE Junior School, Alverstoke

Survival In The Night

M ining for ores, to craft a sword.

I 'll mine all night and then I'll fight.

N ever mind now, the mobs are out.

E vil zombies and skeletons attack.

C raft a sword to fight off the creepers.

R unning through the trees the creepers are chasing me.

A ttack before they blow up.

F ort made of wood with a bedrock bunker.

T oo late to fight, it is now midnight.

Arthur Westmorland (8)

Alverstoke CE Junior School, Alverstoke

Minecraft

M inerals are something you can find underground.

I find things like gold, iron and diamonds.

N ever put redstone and TNT together.

E at animals to stay alive.

C are for others and share well.

R egenerating your health can be hard on survival!

A nimals are my favourite thing.

F inding monster spawners can be rare.

T eamwork and sharing gets you much further.

Issy Dodd (7)

Alverstoke CE Junior School, Alverstoke

Halloween

In the misty churchyard dark and grey,
Ghosts and ghouls arise to terrorise this day,
Vampires, werewolves come out to scare,
Will you go near them, would you dare?
Sweets and candy are a Halloween treat,
Lots of lovely delights to eat,
Lantern pumpkins glimmer in the night,
Carved like bats to give you a fright,
As the spooky night draws to an end,
The ghosts and ghouls to their graves descend.

Ethan Powell (8)
Alverstoke CE Junior School, Alverstoke

The Big Match

Sunday morning goals need scoring
So off to football we go
With smiles on our faces and fire in our bellies
We wait for the whistle to blow
Running like a cheetah up and down the wing
I never give up, I really want to win
A kick from the goalie
It lands at my feet
I take on a player and then *boom*, goal!
The crowd go wild, they scream and shout
Another great win without a doubt.

Alfred William Gibbs (8)

Alverstoke CE Junior School, Alverstoke

My Minecraft World

M y world on Minecraft

I s very hard to survive

N ight-time is the hardest

E vents and challenges are hard

C rafting with stone is fun

R unning away and killing people is challenging

A fter you are armed up

F ighting Endermen is what I do

T eaming up with online friends is the best

Now why don't you have a go?

Connor Mark Stephen Cassese (8)

Alverstoke CE Junior School, Alverstoke

Minecraft

M ining, crafting, building, playing
I t's time to get an Iron Golem guard
N ether is dangerous, so is the Ender
E lytras fly with a fireworks display
C rafting table, very useful
R unning, walking, flying fast or slow
A mazing things to play and do
F abulous display of everything on Minecraft
T aming wolves and ocelots.

Jemima Nottingham (7)
Alverstoke CE Junior School, Alverstoke

My Family

M ummy and Daddy are special because they care about me.

Y esterday, Mummy helped me with my homework.

F unny phone calls with Daddy make me laugh.

A mazing treats and holidays are fun.

M ummy and Daddy are special because they make me happy.

I am grateful for them both.

L ove is shared in our home.

Y ay for my mummy and daddy!

Willow Humphries (8)

Alverstoke CE Junior School, Alverstoke

Friendship

F riends are kind and loving.

R ose is my best friend.

I ntelligent friends are good.

E very friend is lovely.

N ever be mean to a good friend.

D ulcie is an amazing friend.

S ophie is a good musician and friend.

H elp your best friend when they're hurt.

I sla is a nice friend.

P hoebe can be a great friend.

Willow Sellers (8)
Alverstoke CE Junior School, Alverstoke

Eat, Sleep, Mine, Repeat!

Minecraft can be creative,
Mythical creatures exist,
I like that there are dogs!
The diamond block makes things look fancy,
You can use a diamond sword to destroy things,
Eat, sleep, mine, repeat!

Cyan is a good colour to use,
Use your imagination!
My favourite mob is a sheep,
It's a good game,
Minecraft is epic!
Eat, sleep, mine, repeat.

Freddie Jeeves (7)
Alverstoke CE Junior School, Alverstoke

A Journey Into Space!

S aturn has the biggest rings,
P luto is a dwarf,
A steroids are big and small,
C an you see any planets in the sky?
E ven Lego has gone into space,

A re there other creatures out there?
L et us go to Mars soon,
I t can be hard in space,
E nd the journey now,
N ow let's have a rest from space.

Troy John Wadsworth (8)
Alverstoke CE Junior School, Alverstoke

Rotten Romans' Lunch!

Rotten Romans, what a yucky bunch,
You wouldn't believe what they had for lunch.
Like a pig brains and guts from rotten fish,
Slimy cow udders was another favourite dish.
Poor little dormice would get dipped in honey,
Then they would all end up in a rotten Roman's
tummy.
Rotten Romans lay down as they ate so quick,
They scoffed and scoffed till they were sick!

Amelia Philbrow (8)
Alverstoke CE Junior School, Alverstoke

Building Blocks

Minecraft is about building houses, villages and a valley,
Minecraft monsters hide in the alley,
You can fight the monsters with a sword,
Keep on playing and you will never get bored.

You can play Minecraft at night or day,
You can invite your friends to come and play,
Friends can build houses and worlds with you,
Also building roller coasters too.

Erin Isobel Morgan (7)
Alverstoke CE Junior School, Alverstoke

Creature Time

There is this huge game,
That is driving me insane,
It is full of fierce creatures,
With furry features.

Who is this creature,
With the furry features,
Walking in my village?
I hope he doesn't see us.

If we all run and hide,
The creature with furry features,
Will not be able to reach us,
And will not be able to eat us.

Lily Rose Gray-Goddard (8)
Alverstoke CE Junior School, Alverstoke

My Love Of Lego

I have Lego girls,
One has a lot of curls,
I have Lego ice creams,
They are fun and make me scream.

I have two Lego cars,
Olivia loves studying the stars,
My little sister wants me to share,
But I don't care.

I play Lego for hours,
While building princess towers,
Lego is my thing,
Let's see what Santa brings.

Megan Pink (7)
Alverstoke CE Junior School, Alverstoke

I Love Football

I love football, it's fun in the sun,
Exciting in the rain,
But then sometimes a pain,
Running, kicking, passing, shooting, booting
Shorts, socks and shirts,
My number: 10, beating a player called Ben,
Goalposts, green field, jumping over a hole,
Scoring a goal,
Football makes me feel happy and great,
I wish I could get past number eight.

George Rondeau (8)
Alverstoke CE Junior School, Alverstoke

I See The Sea

S uper, shiny waves.
E very day it's in the same place.
A lways fun to play at.

S plashing happily in the sea.
E very wave crashes.
A good view is the sea.

S ummer, the best time to be in the sea.
E normous, blue, clam-filled sea.
A lways makes me feel happy.

Matthew Stephenson (7)

Alverstoke CE Junior School, Alverstoke

Football

Football is the best,
It's better than the rest,
Running down the wing,
To pass the ball in.

Football is the best,
It's ahead of the rest,
When you play as a team,
You must not be mean.

Football is the best,
You can control the ball on your chest,
When I play to win,
I try to score top bins.

Jude Last (7)
Alverstoke CE Junior School, Alverstoke

Daisy Dog

D aisy pulls on a walk,
A nd she wishes she could talk,
I like to hug her every hour,
S he has a name that's a flower,
Y ou'll be surprised, she'll blow your mind,

D aisy is a dog that's friendly and kind,
O ur dog is the world's best,
G o on, put her to the test.

Dominic Darling (7)
Alverstoke CE Junior School, Alverstoke

Cream Of The Crop

Dig, dig, dig, smash, smash, smash,
Blocks made to build or crash.

Great designs made by me,
I've made it all from a house to a tree.

Build some fruit, maybe a mango,
Come to my channel 'Charlie Tango'.

Now it's time to battle my way to the top,
Minecraft is the cream of the crop!

Coral-Tai Lock (7)
Alverstoke CE Junior School, Alverstoke

My Minecraft

M y Minecraft house is really cool.

I love Minecraft!

N ever challenge a creeper to a fight.

E xciting landscapes.

C raft your dream.

R emember, don't walk into dark, gloomy caves!

A dvanced techniques!

F lowers and trees and planting things.

T otally imaginary?

William Shepherd (7)

Alverstoke CE Junior School, Alverstoke

Minecraft Is My Craft!

Minecraft helps you see in the dark,
Crafting the game and building an ark.

Minecraft is a dream come true,
Building a house and something new.

Pat and Jen and Stumpy too,
Excitement brewing and giving a clue.

Minecraft is my craft, I'll tell you now...
Ballistic Squid has shown me how!

Noah Walton-Carr (7)
Alverstoke CE Junior School, Alverstoke

Minecraft Fun

Build a diamond and a gold sword,
Travelling day and night,
Creepers coming in their hordes,
I'm ready to fight,
Drinking potions for jump, speed and night vision,
Craft things? Break things?
What a decision,
Build a city so big,
Kill all the pigs,
Go to work under the oak tree,
Blow everything up with TNT.

Harvey Pout (7)
Alverstoke CE Junior School, Alverstoke

Minecraft Mobs

M obs in Minecraft give you a fright,
 I f you see them, put up a fight.
N etler in the night,
 E ndermen's plight.
C raft a light that is bright,
R abbits run out of sight.
A lex reaches a great height,
 F riends look after you in the twilight,
T hey hold you tight.

Harry Panther (8)

Alverstoke CE Junior School, Alverstoke

Blocks

M ini blocks below,

I nventing ways to stow.

N ever getting caught,

E nder can't use his port.

C rafting through the big blocks,

R andom skies and realm blocks.

A mazing YouTubers build impressive sites,

F or DanTDM and Stampy to have an epic fight.

T DM wins!

Noah Samuel Whitbread (7)

Alverstoke CE Junior School, Alverstoke

Swimming

S ticky swim cap

W etsuit in the sea to keep warm

I like swimming because it's fun

M y heart beats fast and I feel excited

M uppets on the radio in the car

I jump into the pool, I make a big splash

N ervous when I go on my back

G oing home to eat Welsh cakes.

Niamh O'Meara (7)

Alverstoke CE Junior School, Alverstoke

My Hobby

M y hobby is swimming
Y esterday and today in the pool

H oping I am good at lots of things in swimming
O range and all kinds of colours of swimming costumes
B lack and blue hats and white too
B eautiful butterflies on costumes
Y ellow swim shorts, I don't wear.

Erin Rose Willis (7)

Alverstoke CE Junior School, Alverstoke

My Brother

M y brother is William and he is nine
Y es, he is amazing!

B rilliant friend
R acing on water, he's a good sailor
O ften on the Xbox
T oo, too cool
H e is precious to me
E very day he makes us laugh
R eally good fun, I love him.

Hannah Groom (7)
Alverstoke CE Junior School, Alverstoke

Dolphin

D arting through the sparkling seas
O ceans are crossed on its travels
L eaping over the glittering waves
P utting the precious pearl in the clam
H earing the vibrations of his flippers
I nviting his dolphin friends to play
N eeding a rest before the new day.

Isla Valentine Harris (8)

Alverstoke CE Junior School, Alverstoke

The Magical Slime Rhyme Poem

The slime glitters in the night
Let's hope it isn't too bright
Because if it is
It might give you a fright
The magic in the slime is all mine
It can turn itself into red wine
Given plenty of time
I shall have enough to dine
PS: My mummy will then be drunk all the time.

Sophie Brown (7)
Alverstoke CE Junior School, Alverstoke

Books

Big books, small books, tall books, short books,
Fact books, story books, dictionary,
Old books, new books, any books will do.
IPods, crime books, iPhone, notebook,
And other stuff will not do.
Homework books are not for me,
Instead I'll have spaghetti for tea and hot
chocolate please!

Jack Allibone (8)
Alverstoke CE Junior School, Alverstoke

My Friends

My friends are very nice.

Me and my friends every now and then play with dice.

My friends are very kind but have also brilliant minds.

We always have a good play.

We don't care if it's a cold winter's day.

My friends are nice when I'm feeling sad.

My friends are never bad.

Isobel Violet De-Pass (7)

Alverstoke CE Junior School, Alverstoke

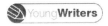

Volcanoes

I hear rumbling all around,
Rocks are tumbling to the ground.
Crash! Bang! Boom! down they go,
Now the boiling lava will flow.

Lava feeling as hot as the sun,
Comes shooting out so quickly, run!
Down the crater I will dash,
Around the rocks and burning ash.

George White (7)
Alverstoke CE Junior School, Alverstoke

Spike

My pet lizard, Spike
He is my very best friend
He is yellow, brown, black and white
His skin is scaly, his toes are long
His tail is fat to keep him strong
He walks along his sandy hide
He has rocks, trees and sand
He would like to eat the fattest mealworm in the land.

Thomas Withers (8)

Alverstoke CE Junior School, Alverstoke

Friends

F orever they play in the day.

R espect others.

I magination helps them believe and learn.

E verlasting friendship forever.

N ice children always make good friends.

D ifferent doesn't matter.

S unshine shines over good people.

Phoebe May Smith (8)

Alverstoke CE Junior School, Alverstoke

Blocks

B uilding is so much fun but bedrock you can't break.

L adders bring you up in the sky.

O celots are very fast when you feed them.

C reepers explode like a firework.

K illing skeletons get you bones.

S limes are big, bouncy and slimy.

Jasmine Stone (7)

Alverstoke CE Junior School, Alverstoke

Unicorns Are Real

In the sky
Unicorns fly
Painting rainbows
As they go by.

Glistening bright
What a wonderful sight
Making dreams come true
All through the night.

Magical forces
Candyfloss sauces
Have you even seen
Such wonderful horses?

Jessica Lewis (7)
Alverstoke CE Junior School, Alverstoke

Singing

S inging out loud and proud.

I nventing your own words and rhymes.

N ice doing it with your friends.

G etting a good feeling inside.

I nteresting singing in different ways.

N ever forget your words.

G rooving to the melody.

Holly Jones-Cassidy (7)

Alverstoke CE Junior School, Alverstoke

My House

I'm going to build a house today,
I want to build it quick.
I'm going to get my pickaxe,
To mine the perfect bricks.

I'm going to use diamond blocks,
And some Ender stone.
I hope when I'm digging,
I don't find a crunchy bone.

Jayden Ruff (8)
Alverstoke CE Junior School, Alverstoke

Seasons

S weet summer sun,

E njoying the summer fun,

A ll the leaves are falling down,

S lowly turning yellow, red and brown,

O ne early winter's morning,

N othing was to be seen but snow falling,

S pring has sprung at last!

Lily Adams (8)
Alverstoke CE Junior School, Alverstoke

Unicorns

U nicorns soar through the sky!
N icely waving their rainbow tails!
I ndependent of magic.
C areful with what they do.
O h, they are beautiful.
R unning happily in the sun!
N icely loving.
S ometimes sleepy.

Olivia Keen (7)
Alverstoke CE Junior School, Alverstoke

My Friend Ben

Ben, my friend, is good with the kisses.
When I go out it's me that he misses.
He likes his food and loves a nice treat.
He snores very loudly when he's asleep.
He's cuddly and fun and talks a lot too.
He loves his walks and would love to meet you.

Lara Hooper (9)
Alverstoke CE Junior School, Alverstoke

Playing Rugby

R unning fast and scoring zigzag tries,

U nderstanding the rules and beating the other team,

G rabbing tags and defending my line,

B eing with my friends and having lots of fun,

Y ellow and blue are the bright colours of my shirt.

Nancy Rose Smith (7)

Alverstoke CE Junior School, Alverstoke

Titanic

T itanic is my name,

I hold lots of people,

T itanic is my name,

A ship full of stuff,

N ot enough lifeboats,

I ceberg dead ahead!

C hildren and women first,

Titanic was my name.

Isobel Macaulay (7)
Alverstoke CE Junior School, Alverstoke

Swimming

Gliding through the water,
One arm after the other.
Gliding through the water,
My legs go kick, kick, kick!
Gliding through the water,
I'm blowing bubbles from my mouth.
Gliding into the water,
I can't wait to swim again.

Owen Piner (8)

Alverstoke CE Junior School, Alverstoke

Minecraft With My Dad

With tools in hand we mine deeper,
We hunt for diamonds but avoid creepers,
My dad's a noob and always tries,
But falling in lava, he always dies,
With many blocks from many biomes,
We head to the furnace to build our Minecraft homes.

Luke Williams (7)

Alverstoke CE Junior School, Alverstoke

Special Dreams

D reams are fun and adventurous
R unning around on adventures
E veryone is involved in dreams
A dream can be whatever you make it
M ade up of real-life thoughts
S o sleep and dream.

Leigha Lisa Davis (9)

Alverstoke CE Junior School, Alverstoke

Cricket

C atch it, catch it.

R oot bowled for ninety.

I ndia vs England.

C ould England lose?

K eep the faith!

E ngland win by twenty runs.

T omorrow you'll be on the pitch.

Ben Brett (9)

Alverstoke CE Junior School, Alverstoke

My Little Fish

My little fish loves to swim.
My little fish is safe from fishermen.
My little fish named Peachade.
My little fish taps on the tank.
My little fish watches the flakes bob.
My little fish, cleaning his tank is my job.

Evie Speight (8)
Alverstoke CE Junior School, Alverstoke

The Great

I run as fast as I can,
Dribbling with my feet,
Someone comes to tackle me,
But I'm not easy to beat,
I look up at the goal,
Shoot and score,
Then throw myself on the floor,
The crowd are in awe.

Jacob Jay Taulbut (8)
Alverstoke CE Junior School, Alverstoke

The Brown Bone Coat

The stone was brown
And went to town
A superhero is a boat
And had a brown coat.

The superhero found the stone
Went home, got a bone
And now he has a brown bone coat.

Kiera Fryer (7)
Alverstoke CE Junior School, Alverstoke

My Soccer Dream

I ran with the ball
And tried to score.
I tried not to fall
Or land on the floor.
I ran, ran and tried to be fast,
My aim was to shoot
And not be last.
Goal!

Kieran Yinhu Richardson (7)
Alverstoke CE Junior School, Alverstoke

Mining

M ining is my friend

  I t is my life

N ot my enemy

  I find diamonds

N ext time I will do better

G ood times happen.

Logan James Hall (10)

Alverstoke CE Junior School, Alverstoke

The Day Of The Dead!

There was a boy called Carlos,
Who lived in Mexico and it was All Hallows' Eve.
He and his friends had finished telling scary stories
And Carlos exclaimed, 'Those were scary!'
One day later, Carlos was ready for Halloween.
Dark was the night, Halloween was here
And I saw a deer who said,
'Oh no! It is a g-g-ghost!'

The ghost was chasing Carlos.
Carlos went back to his house,
He was nearly safe.
The ghost passed the garden gnome,
As it was imagining ruling Rome.
The gnome broke the windows.

Nearly morning, 'I need a pumpkin,' exclaimed
Carlos.
He made its eyes and a creepy mouth.
He put a torch in it, showed it to the ghost
And said, 'I'm not scared of you.'

Ali Bunnett (9)
New Milton Junior School, New Milton

Minecraft Love Poem

Every day I'm falling deeper,
I stalk you like a creeper,
Nothing can keep me away.
Enderman better stay away.
I'll travel to the Nether for you,
I'd kill the Ender Dragon for you.
I started with ten hearts to spare,
But now I couldn't really care.
The only heart that's critical is the one I give you.
I have travelled deserts, plains and seas,
Not in the day but in the night,
You may see zombies come out to fight,
If you are careful you'll see,
They cannot catch you while you flee.
If you are not careful, they will attack
And try to jump onto your back.
One will try to take your brain,
With it there will be a zombie reign.
When a zombie is in sight,
You must do what you think is right.

Punch him in his face
And tell him he is a really big disgrace.

Molly James-Croft (10)
New Milton Junior School, New Milton

Days At Minecraft

Minecraft blocks are not all shapes and sizes,
Only squares.
Two bricks look like pairs.
You can get all animals;
Pink or blue, mushroom cows, woo-hoo!
Enemies are everywhere,
Enderman, Enderman, get out of his way,
Do not be his prey.

Mine through the night, watch out,
Zombies in sight.
Make a village, maybe on a hill,
Just please get your fill.
Creepy caves near,
Watch out for scary noises to hear,
Like witches that are evil,
First you need some food to fill.

Night-time passes as the days go,
Go on a hill now.
A loud humming noise,
You'd better take some torches, boys.

Daytime's here, trees near.
Make some weapons,
Oh no, need to run.
First, let's look at the snow,
Then bye-bye, I have to go.

Maddie Hendy (10)
New Milton Junior School, New Milton

Hostile Mobs In A Nutshell

Zombies, zombies, on the attack,
If you hurt them, they'll get you back.

Creepers, creepers, like a bomb,
Losers weapons, now my inventory's gone.

Spiders, spiders, in the cave,
Stone so thick, you simply can't save.

Skeletons, skeletons, wielding bows and arrows,
You can't kill them because they're so narrow.

Zombie pigmen in the Nether,
Hiding within a fortress,
Too scary where I doubt you'll endeavour.

Ghosts, ghosts, seem friendly at last,
Looming in the air, ready for a blast.

Sammy Lillington (9)
New Milton Junior School, New Milton

Mooshroom!

This is the day I saw the surprise...
When suddenly I got a moo for a prize.
It was a cow with two mushrooms on top,
But looked like a mooing mushroom of course!
We tried calling it a mushroom, a moo-mush and a
moo-mushroom,
But then we called it a mooshroom.
Finally, a perfect name fitted with mush, a room
and a moo.
Hooray, hooray! There it is!
Feed it some pork, feed it some hay!
For goodness' sake. Hooray!
Well, of course we got it right,
For the good things of course come again at the
end of the day.
Well, happy moo-year!

Weronika Ewa Marciniak (8)
New Milton Junior School, New Milton

Creeps In The Dens, Creeps Never End

Creepers to the right, creepers to the left,
Creepers all behind, creepers never end.
Pigs in the den, they will never end.
Creepers, creepers in their den,
Almost to their end.
Creepers look like trees,
But they walk around like fleas.
Creepers may be in your dreams,
But they're not actually.
Creepers in hiding so they don't get caught,
The creepers hide because if they don't, they will meet their end.
Pigs love jigs and stay in their den,
So if it rains, they'll stay dry until the end.

Alice Green (7)
New Milton Junior School, New Milton

Minecraft Moments

Don't lose a life now,
Meat and leather on the ground,
Blocks, blocks and more blocks,
Axes in your hand and fire all around.

Zombies and skeletons come to life,
Make a note on where to hide,
Collect more, claim more, make a great big house,
Candlelit tracks and trails set, more and more to come.

Survival, weapons, much, much more,
Wood to bricks, meat to plants,
Spooky spiderwebs just like string,
Waiting for an adventure to begin...

Martha Westaway (9)
New Milton Junior School, New Milton

How To Make Gold

How to make gold
You wonder how to make gold
You need to get some mud, brick, stone and coal.

You need to get a bowl and put the mud into it.
Then you need to put the coal into it with the mud
And then stir it.

After you mix it, you put in the brick
But you still need to mix it.

Then you need to put the stone in
Then mix it for five minutes.

Put the mixture in the oven for five hours
Here you go, gold!

Elif Stamcheva (7)
New Milton Junior School, New Milton

Animal Friendly

In the night I see the moonlight in sight.
All of a sudden, a bunny jumped in my arms
And a fox called Mox tried to bite the bunny's tail.
I said, 'No! Don't do that!'
So I hit Mox on his little head.
Why is he such a pot of angriness?
Why can't he be like fish and a crab,
They like each other,
Or a worm and a maggot?
I wonder why foxes and rabbits don't like each other.
I wonder what other animals don't like each other.

Allana Hendry (8)
New Milton Junior School, New Milton

The Power Of Imagination

Swish, swish, swish, swirl, through the portal you go
Find a land of sweets, ice cream and cookies
Meet the fantasies of truth... your imagination
It's a place to let your imagination run wild
Make an imaginary friend come to life
Play Minecraft, watch films and even ride roller coasters
Sleep all day and boogie all night long
You'll never get bored, this palace of wonder is evergreen.

Romilly Lewis (9)
New Milton Junior School, New Milton

Finding Something New

Redstone is red,
Lapis is blue,
If you go mining,
You'll find something new.
Oh, what is this,
So shiny and bright?
It's an emerald all green,
What a delight.
Then down in the cave,
I get a fright as a...
Zombie approaches into the light.
I pick up my sword
And cut off his leg,
He falls into the lava,
I run home and live happily ever after.

Katie Gazzard (9)
New Milton Junior School, New Milton

The Enderman

Eyes will blind you,
May I remind you,
My teleportation will freak you.

My skinny arms,
The way I move,
Will certainly destroy you.

For your own safety,
Wear a pumpkin,
It will keep you healthy.

I drop Ender pearls,
Will take you in whirls,
Let you teleport like me,
Oh, however will that be?

Reanna Rarela (8)
New Milton Junior School, New Milton

Fun Friendship

Friends make you happy.
Friends make you smile.
They make things better if only for a while.

Laughing out loud.
Such a joy.
Like playing with your favourite toy.

Laugh or giggle.
So much fun.
Together we are number one.

Oi, you heard me say you're my friend.
Will you stay and play with me today?

Alissa Carroll (8)
New Milton Junior School, New Milton

Changing Seasons

Dainty, crispy leaves,
Like long-lost friends moving house,
Chattering softly.

Strong sunrays calling,
Round and round, circling us,
Day comes, evening falls.

Snowflakes giggling,
Crunchy snow rolling,
Tall snowman melting.

Pink flowers growing,
Lambs being born,
Cold, whispering air.

Ruby Jenner (9)
New Milton Junior School, New Milton

Summertime

The sun is the light, boiling hot today,
Faster and faster, the marathon runners run away.
Everyone cheers as the winner runs,
Everybody eats a bun.
Ladies sunbathe in the summer sun,
Meanwhile, people run into the sun.
People lick their ice cream away,
The sun sets on another day.

Eva Costello (7)
New Milton Junior School, New Milton

The Sword

Chop up pigs,
With your diamond sword.
Block your enemies,
With your iron sword.
Attack the Ender Dragon,
With your golden sword.
Stab fierce zombies,
With your wooden sword.
Kill the Wither,
With your stone sword.
Let your adventures run wild,
With your sword.

Charles Peacock (9)
New Milton Junior School, New Milton

The Mine In Minecraft

Mine in the deep, dark mine
Digging up emeralds and diamonds
Gold and all sorts of ore.

Attacking mobs till
Daylight has shown
Mine every day
Armour will show.

Mining is fun
Especially with your friends
Have a mine day
Mining is fun.

Olivia Elizabeth McCracken (7)
New Milton Junior School, New Milton

Minecraft Story

Haiku poetry

Minecraft is so fun
Weapons, diamonds, emerald blocks
Minecart tracks, awesome.

Zombies fight people
Zombies eat pigs, cows, chickens
Zombie pigs eat pigs.

Steve is awesome
A good team means good players
Steve's a good player.

Emma Rebbecca Hall (9)
New Milton Junior School, New Milton

Mobs-Rhyme

Creeper! Creeper!
Don't come out
Stay in hiding
Don't creep out.

Zombie! Zombie!
Burns at day
But when it's night
It's not afraid.

Enderman! Enderman!
Teleports around
Hates the daytime
Screams around.

Ellen Hiscott (9)
New Milton Junior School, New Milton

Building

Building bricks are what you need
I build towers, walls and castles
To stop baddies from getting me.
Let's build to live.
Doing craft is my thing, so let's build.
I build to become a master builder,
Never give up,
Give it a go,
So let's build.

Ryker Augustine (8)
New Milton Junior School, New Milton

Weird And Wonderful World

We went to the beach
And took my pet leech.
We went to sea and found a pea
I took it back home
And sold it alone
Until he lost it
And found the hostage
And now it's time
For this poem to end
Hopefully, I won't go
Round the bend!

Harvey Brown (8)
New Milton Junior School, New Milton

Dark Pie

Mining town,
The night creepers are in sight.
Run, hide, or you will be pie.
If you survive, run back home
And make a pie of your own.
Crusty on top, soft inside,
Made just right to go inside.
Tummy rumble, makes a noise,
Yummy, yummy, lovely pie.

Charlie Michael Hooper (8)
New Milton Junior School, New Milton

In The Dead Of Night

The devil will be in your head
Till the day, the day you're dead.
Blood on your bed,
Fears in your head,
Bones when you're dead.
They'll want to be fed.
'Murder, crime, a horrible time...'
Voices whimper, wispy and fine.

Lily Mays (10)
New Milton Junior School, New Milton

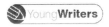

In The Deep Blue Sea

Mermaids swim touching water,
Crabs scuttle along the floor,
Fish swim amongst the coral,
Seaweed sways in the current.
Seagulls circle looking for a snack,
Oysters keep their treasure safe.
What would you do if you lived in the sea?

Megan Guppy (7)
New Milton Junior School, New Milton

Morning Scares

Under my bed
A monster jumped
It went and ate my boiled egg
Also it had Meg as a feast.
The monster was a hairy beast
It screeched loud
And reached for me.
It might get you too
But first it will need to go to the loo.

Maisie Wardle (8)
New Milton Junior School, New Milton

Daydream

I dreamed, dreamed and dreamed,
All day long.
In my dream I saw a big, beautiful butterfly
With colourful, long wings.
I tried to catch it but it kept on flying.
Dreams are like butterflies.

Mia Bibin (8)
New Milton Junior School, New Milton

Chocolate

Chocolate is so nice
If you agree with me
Shout out loud
For glee.

Maltesers are brilliant
And crunchy too.

Lydia Buswell (8)
New Milton Junior School, New Milton

The Life I Lead

Late, late one cold winter's night,
When the lamp post shone extremely bright,
I lay curled up tight in a ball,
Resting my back on a crumbling wall.
The life I lead has a worthless fate,
The life I lead is the life I hate.

In the workhouse I lie, brave and bold,
Hidden in a wooden crate and a blanket old.
I dream of tomorrow, running away,
Living on the streets, becoming a stray.
The life I lead is a fight for survival,
The life I lead is the life of death's arrival.

Warm by the blaze of the fire I sleep,
Next to my tonnes of siblings forming a mountain
heap.
The room we live in is the one we share,
We have no furniture, it's completely bare.
The life I lead is a repetitive day,
The life I lead is a life with no sun at bay.

Tonight I lie in bed awake,
Thinking of other children's sake.
Even though I'm rich and need nothing more,
I'm always thinking of the poor.
The life I lead is full of compassion,
The life I lead is the life in fashion.

I am Alice, the Queen's second daughter,
The palace days I would love to slaughter.
My mother runs round pretending she's boss
And my sisters act like they're as sweet as
candyfloss.
The life I lead is the one all adore,
The life I lead is the life of more.

We are all different in precious ways,
Have different lives and different days.
However, at the end of the game,
We are all people and they are the same.
The lives we lead are built with a different
technique,
The lives we lead are lives specially unique.

Ffion Turberfield (10)

Preston Candover Primary School, Preston Candover

In The Palace

Why am I here?
With a fear
Of the bobbies
And their torturing hobbies.

Happy families live and play
And their children spit and say,
'You'll never get a job in the palace,'
Then they kick me with malice!

I look through the windows,
Children laugh and the mother sews,
A boy looks up and sees me hurting,
He walks to the window and closes the curtain.

I kick at the ground,
What have I found?
A five pound note,
But I cannot gloat.

If the other boys see,
They'll take it from me!

I'll apply for a job,
I'm so happy, I start to sob!

I jump in a blanket of snow,
the next day I will go:
I will get a job in the palace,
I'll show those boys who kicked me with malice.

Guess what? I've got a job,
No more will I cry and sob.
Now I serve her royal highness, the Queen,
But you'll never guess what I have seen.

An Indian man called Abdul caught her eye,
Made one single tear trickle, made her cry.
The day that Victoria's life was sold,
A lot of trouble began to unfold.

That one single man who caught her eye,
That one single man who made her cry,
But that doesn't matter, I am still here,
Serving the king, not Vicky dear.

Sorry Vicky, we respect you,
From the evening dusk to the morning dew!

Thank you, Vicky, you changed our land,
From the Scotland snows to the Cornwall sands.

Izzy Richardson (10)
Preston Candover Primary School, Preston Candover

My Past

My clammy hands are harshly burning,
I'm so dizzy, the floor is turning.
I see a lady holding a baby,
Is it me with my mother? Maybe.
Now there's a man! I can see him too!
And now he is looking at me and starting to coo.
My past is lost, I want to stay,
Please, please, please, don't take me away.
I walk in the streets to get some air,
Wait! Who's that? She has my hair!
She embraces me, I push her away,
I don't want to look at her,
I don't want to stay.
'Wait, John!' I hear my name.
I turn around, it's all the same.
My past is lost, should I fight?
Shall I bring it back with all my might?

Evie James (10)
Preston Candover Primary School, Preston Candover

As The Fire Blazes At Night

On a Friday night, they say, when the moon is
behind a cloud,
London streets are silent, all but dogs that howl
aloud.
The road is as bare as a desert, and finally
footsteps appear;
The owner of the manor is coming back from his
well-earned career.

He knocks on the door in the darkness and waits
for the answer to come,
And there is a dark-shaped shadow; his wife stands
cross and glum.
At one o'clock in the morning, he stomps up with
an aching head,
Therefore, after being so exhausted, he
immediately goes to bed.

He woke up, still very late at night, with a wisp of
smoke to his nose,
He ran downstairs to the kitchen, but stopped as
an orange flame rose!

So the firemen came in the first ray of sun when
day was beginning to break,
But when put out, the air kept wobbling, like the
ripples on a vast blue lake.

Now they picked wallets from all rich men, and
if caught, they had to lie,
But one day they had no strength to stand up, so
they are forced to curl up and die.
And on a ghostly night, they say, when the moon is
behind a cloud,
London streets are silent, all but dogs that howl
aloud.

A man knocks on the darkness and waits for the
answer to come
And there is a dark-shaped shadow; his wife stands
cross and glum.
They stare at each other for a moment, each one a
mournful refrain,
But whatever happened a few nights ago, will
never happen again.

Thomas Gray (10)
Preston Candover Primary School, Preston Candover

A Forgotten Memory

I feel sick, my stomach is churning,
My thoughts are lost and my mind is turning.
'Argh!' a never-ending scream,
Where was it coming from? What does it mean?
I run and I race, following that sound,
I grit my teeth before my heart starts to pound.
Round the corner, down an alleyway,
'Get back here right now! I'll make you pay!'

An angry little girl, sat in a heap on the floor,
'Oh come on! I can't stand it any more!
My dress is ruined and I've lost my toy,
Go after him! Go get that boy!'
I can hear footsteps, he's definitely near,
A shadow; he's tall and dangerous (that's clear).
I am out of breath, my lungs are burning,
Am I out of time? My head is twirling.
'Aha, an iron rod in the gutter,
I might be able to use it,' I quietly mutter.
I creep out from the darkness and into the light,
I'm ready, well, I think I'm ready to fight.
A dead end, there's no way out!

However, in my head, an idea starts to sprout.
A crowbar in hand and a window full of toys,
Whack! Smash! I've lost all poise!
A beautiful teddy bear, a fuzzy feeling,
A dark red tag... Jack Smith stealing.
That's me! Jack Smith is my name!
Then I remember all I feel is pain...

Mimi Jones (10)

Preston Candover Primary School, Preston Candover

Dear Diary

Dear Diary,

I'm going to tell you of the Victorian time,
When my poor life was a crime.
No clothes, baths or scrumptious food,
All the policemen in an impatient mood.

I was living on the ghostly streets,
With nothing but a few dirty sheets.
All the people passing by,
Took no notice, shooed me away like a fly.

I was poor, there was no doubt about that,
I wasn't as important as a rich lady's cat.
She lived in a big house across the road,
Owning a white horse who always pulled her load.

Every day she would stop and give me food,
While people watched in amazement and booed.
She would always give me a friendly smile,
Which made me happy, for a while.

Then one day she stopped next to me,
She exclaimed,
'Come in and have some warm tea!'

I could not resist, I had to go in,
When I drank from a cup, I had to grin.
I felt the warm liquid roll down in my body,
'You can stay if you want.'
Finally, I had somebody!

So that's what I did and here I am,
Sitting on a velvet chair, her little lamb.
I get washed, fed and dressed with care,
I love the old brick house that we share.

Jane Lang-Horgan (10)
Preston Candover Primary School, Preston Candover

I Live On The Streets

I strike around the streets of London,
Sleeping on rooftops, from the bobbies we run.
No place to go, no place to sleep,
Just pickpocket money without a peep.
Trying to find a decent home,
Rats and foxes on the streets they roam.
Foxes rummage around in the bins,
Eating cans of fish and sardine tins.

Then a smile spreads across my face,
'I've finally found it, this is the place.'
As I walk through the rusty, red doors,
I stop and think about the laws.
Will I be allowed to stay here?
On my pale face, I shed a tear.
Street dogs howling at the winter moon,
I'm dreaming I'll get a pay soon.

I walk inside the giant building,
I'm so unlucky, everyone's laughing.

Scratchy waistcoats and a pinafore dress,
That's what we wear, our faces a mess.
I was chucked out, to the rooftops I return,
Rich people pass without any concern.
Rich people laugh at us poor street children,
Posh ladies, lucky children and happy men.

I live on the streets in a blanket of snow,
I live on the streets, snowballs they throw.
I live on the streets, when the sun's shining down,
I live on the streets in London town.

Charlotte Gent (10)
Preston Candover Primary School, Preston Candover

Livin' On The Streets

Hey, I'm Sam and I live on the streets,
I don't have any bed sheets.
I don't even have a proper bed
And I don't get properly fed.
When I look into rich houses,
I see women in embroidered white blouses.
I ask myself,
How can you afford that shelf?
With books by Shakespeare
And some to make you shiver with fear.
Every night,
I fight,
Death for survival,
Warmth is vital.
I also need,
A good feed,
Fill my belly
With nice, meaty jelly.
I drink from puddles
And sleep in huddles

With my mate,
By the palace gate.
Where I rest,
Rubbish bins are best!
I always dream,
They make me beam!
I dream, I eat masses of candy,
That's lying on the floor, how very handy.
That dish,
Was so delish!
If only,
I weren't so lonely!
All that make-believe,
Makes me feel free,
Like I'm in a coral reef.
If it was real,
Oh, how happy I'd feel.
'Free! Free!'
I'd shout with glee!
If I had a home,
I would not feel alone.

I won't cry,
Because I'll be dry!

Ollie Webb (10)
Preston Candover Primary School, Preston Candover

Chimney Boy

I stumble up that chimney quick,
The chimney brush is really thick,
The old man starts to groan,
I feel like he's left me all alone.
I climb up so quick,
Yet I feel sick.

I had that pain,
It happened again!
I hear the master shouting, 'Get back to work,'
But he doesn't understand, it's such hard work.

It starts to rain,
I give God the blame,
Bang!
I've slipped,
I've landed on my hip.

I'm back in bed,
To rest my sleepy head.

Harry Jones (9)
Preston Candover Primary School, Preston Candover

The Horrible, Horrible Workhouse

Do you want me to tell my story?
Fine, I will but it's very gory.
I used to live on the street,
My heart always skipped a beat.
I tried to sneak into a home,
But the bobbies had come
Because the family had called on the telephone.

I went to the horrible workhouse,
Which had more than one woodlouse.
Queen Victoria everybody adores,
But not me, I'm just poor.
As I work hour by hour,
I lose all my strength and power.
I'm in the worst place you can be at,
I'm treated like a brat.
Every day I feel sad,
But they just say I'm bad.

Once again,
I had pain

Every day I collected sticks
And went up the chimney
Trying to dodge crumbling bricks.
Suddenly, I ran quick,
I was sick.
I looked down on the floor,
That second matron shouted at me,
She didn't care for the poor.

I wanted to go,
But there was too much snow.
Queen Victoria sits on her throne,
But I'm just alone.
In the workhouse I lay,
Thinking about my terrible day.

Tom Loftus (9)
Preston Candover Primary School, Preston Candover

The Coal Mine

Whilst the coal waters my eyes,
I feel like I want to take to the skies.
The trees above rustle my hair
And I begin to feel the hot, hot air.
I look in disgust at a big, fat man
And then he starts eating from a very big pan.
I walk across the boulders
And jump on people's shoulders.

I climb up high
And find myself high in the sky!
I try not to look down
But I can't resist, then I frown.
I find myself not high at all,
It's now less than a metre, very small!
I jump back down and it hurts a bit,
The master shouts, 'Get back here, Pip!'

The sun is blazing to the ground,
I start to listen to a giant sound!
The sound is the workhouse, lots of smoke I see,
Then I see a dog, I think it likes me.

I stroke the dog,
And he tumbles over a log.
I say goodbye
And he begins to cry.

I break the hard coal
And feel scared down to my soul.
I begin to die,
'Please save me!' I cry...

Oliver Whittle (9)
Preston Candover Primary School, Preston Candover

The Chimney Sweep!

My tearful eyes are full of soot,
While the unstable bricks crumble beneath my
foot.
My ears hear the faint voice below,
In surprise I hear my master bellow:
'Oi, you up there at the top,
Don't you dare disobey me and stop!'
I race to the top of the narrow nightmare,
I see children whose happiness I don't share.
Up the chimney, high I climb,
They might put the fire on, is that a crime?
I'm scared I'm going to fall,
Down, down, like a cannonball.

That night on the rooftops,
Above all the large shops,
I remember my ma told me,
If I see the bobbies to run and flee.
I look down at the street,
I search for something to eat.
I look around and the coppers are here,
Phew! They're arresting two men with some beer.

The next day, up the chimney I go,
I don't know if this time I can put on a show.
This is my life,
This is my story...

Evie Mattia (10)
Preston Candover Primary School, Preston Candover

Rich And Poor Differences

The master of the house sits in his chair,
Awaiting the noises he can't bear.
The children lie in their comfy beds,
With dreams running around in their sleepy heads.
The grand ladies sit brushing their hair,
If they see a child they'll stand and glare.
In the large playroom, the toys are stuffed away,
Waiting for the children to come and play.

The poor children lie on the rooftops
And underneath lay the large shops.
Wondering who they really are,
They hear the drunk men at the bar.
Their illness spreads,
Onto the beds.
All of the small people below,
Looked up and said hello.

One peaceful night,
When it wasn't very bright,
The little children who were pickpockets,
Were stealing lots of little lockets.

They were caught,
Then they were taught,
To run away,
That's now enough for today.

Libby Joanne Crosswell (9)
Preston Candover Primary School, Preston Candover

Chimney Boy

Inside the chimney I climb to the sky,
Reaching way up high.
I see another boy, climbing with a frown,
Across the rooftops not looking down.
The rooftops are rough and tough,
Working as a chimney boy, I've had enough.
The wind brushes across my face,
It's black and dirty, a big disgrace.

I climb down the chimney to see what is wrong,
I fall down the chimney, it took so long.
I see an opening of a door...
Not daring to look at the floor.
I open the door to a street,
Listening to my heart beat.
I see a dog barking like mad,
It makes me feel sad.
I go up to it and say, 'Should I play
With this mysterious stray?'

The ground is covered with a blanket of snow,
I feel sad and cold, it made me low.

My story ends here,
Living in fear.

Leo Bradley Lewis Jackson (9)

Preston Candover Primary School, Preston Candover

Osborne House

The fine quilt's feather lay upon her royal hand,
The sunset full of yellow and pink starts to set
upon my land.
I feel sick, my stomach's turning,
The world of business I am learning.

The last dot placed,
A pang of regret written on my face
Quickly disappeared,
This is where my children will be reared.

Myself and my love entertain thee,
Foreign royalty and ministers come and see.
Fifty years fly by,
I have no reason to lie.

My true love dead,
He bled and bled,
My loneliness overcomes me,
Alone I will be.

In 1861,
I'll never forget this one.

My life spent alone, I know when I die,
We will be reunited again,
I will have no reason to cry.

Oh woe, oh woe.

Isabella Bevilacqua (10)
Preston Candover Primary School, Preston Candover

Sewer Boy

Down in the dark,
Deep underground,
Where rats scurrying
Is the only sound.

Under the roads,
Filled with grime,
The stinking walls,
Smeared with slime.

There lives a boy,
All alone,
The endless tunnels,
His only home.

He once had a life,
A home and a bed,
But now he lives,
Down here instead.

His face is black,
His eyes are grim,
Although he is small,
He is skinny and thin.

He comes up sometimes,
Into the overworld,
Where the sky is grey
And the sun is gold.

Then the bobbies,
Chase him down there,
Where grime and mould,
Sweeten the air.

There lives a boy,
All alone,
The endless sewers,
His only home.

Monty Leonard-Wright (11)
Preston Candover Primary School, Preston Candover

Coal Mines

Wintertime's making me cry,
Inside my rags, wind pushes by.
I get out of bed, I see some snow,
It makes me shiver, I'm feeling really low.

The dove came in making a gust of air,
Carrying food in tins I would love to share.
The wind makes me shiver,
And my bones quiver.

I climb up high,
It gives me the feeling I'm about to die.
I see the stars,
Which makes me feel I'm in Mars.

Crumbly boulders,
Hitting my shoulders.
I run really quick
Which makes me feel sick.

I was in pain,
Once again.

I feel water on my neck,
I hear my master shout, 'Bloomin' heck!'

Charlie Jones (9)

Preston Candover Primary School, Preston Candover

The Chimney Boy

I have no mother and no father,
I would rather die in lava.
My master's called Matt
And he lives in a flat.

Every day is a step to my goal,
So I can escape from this ugly troll!
He makes me feel sad,
But he is very bad!

Every day I climb and climb,
As I watch the ticking time.
I look down and my master said,
'Oi, where's the bread?'

I look down with a smile,
But his face so ugly and vile!
I get back to work,
As I still have a smirk.

I'm now downstairs, I stroke the dog,
I look outside, it looks like a bog.

But I start to cry
And I want to die.

Adam Pugh (9)
Preston Candover Primary School, Preston Candover

Winter

In winter, too scared to sleep,
As thinking of my mother sweep.
Me and my sister hand in hand,
Thinking of who ruled this land.

We climb up to the rooftops,
Looking down on all the shops,
Lizzie is shivering,
While I am quivering.

I am lying on a blanket of snow,
This is my life, it is very low.
My sister's rag,
Has flown away like a bag.

That was my life, it was very low,
I didn't even get to enjoy the snow.

Erin Lawson (10)
Preston Candover Primary School, Preston Candover

But Where Does He Come From?

His hair as messy as a mammoth's fur,
His voice as soft as a cat's purr.
His face as dirty as a devastating bog,
His nails as sharp as those of a dog.

His emotions as wild as a raging boar,
His heart opens from a black door.
His brain filled with sadness,
His heart made with madness.

But where does he come from?

His home is a box,
He sleeps in it like a fox.
He lies on a rag,
Flapping like a flag.

Harry Edward Christopher Seaman (10)
Preston Candover Primary School, Preston Candover

A Night In The Workhouse

I turn, I toss,
I keep thinking of my loss.
Out I get, out of my bed,
Into a room I am led.

The winter moon,
Shone in the room.
The room was extremely bare,
Made my stomach flip in the air.

Only a book,
I went to have a look.
Inside I was sucked, using my imagination,
I wish I was in this creation.

Oliver Coplestone (9)
Preston Candover Primary School, Preston Candover

Grendel!

Death-defying teeth
Blood dripping
Gills like a shark's
Slimy-skinned
Heart-ripper
Angry ogre
Bone-cracker
Knife claws
Horrifying face
Revenge-seeker
Lion mane
Fight-finder.

Nina Acedańska (8)
Preston Candover Primary School, Preston Candover

Grendel

(A kennings poem)

Horrifying demon
Soul-ripper
Flesh-eater
Blood-drinker
Deadly-murderer
Blood-red hands
Swift mover
Warrior-killer
Body-obliterator
Bond-crusher
Tail-whipper.

Harry Jason Corney (8)

Preston Candover Primary School, Preston Candover

Grendel

Death-defying talons
Cursing claws
Darting diminisher
Bloodthirsty
Strong-stringer
Killer of emotions
Lion-headed dagger
Life-haunter
Taunting tail.

Oscar Mattia (8)
Preston Candover Primary School, Preston Candover

Grendel's Mum

(A kennings poem)

Demon queen
Skull-cruncher
Murderous monster
Drool-dripper
Blood-thirsty
Bone-cracker
Hideous beast
Electric hair
Furious phantom.

Willow Pajaree Fannon-Vickery (8)

Preston Candover Primary School, Preston Candover

Hunting

A skin-cutter,
A fighter to death,
A jewel-gleamer,
A fool-catcher,
A night-killer,
A heart-piercer,
A death-thriller,
A fire-thrower.

Lorna Turberfield (8)
Preston Candover Primary School, Preston Candover

The Mighty Grendel
(A kennings poem)

Death-destroyer
Bone-cruncher
Blood-thirsty
Murderous-revenger
Aggressive stingers
Claw-gleamer
Slimy drooler
Drool-dripper.

Raphael Martin-Reynolds (8)
Preston Candover Primary School, Preston Candover

Grendel
(A kennings poem)

Hideous hag
Tin-opener
Silent stalker
Life-stealer
Flesh-eater
Life-hater
Happiness-destroyer
Blood-trooper
Death-defying.

Edward William Corney (8)
Preston Candover Primary School, Preston Candover

Grendel

(A kennings poem)

Hairy mane
Massive fangs
Muscle arms
Monstrous talons
Tail-tangler
Bloodthirsty
Death-dealer
Death-defying eyes.

Noah Taylor (9)

Preston Candover Primary School, Preston Candover

Grendel's Mother

Coral hair
Dreadful dare
Heart-piercer
Blazing claws
Creeping nearer
Jurassic claws
Revenge-seeker
Blood-leaker.

Evie Loftus (8)
Preston Candover Primary School, Preston Candover

Grendel's Mother
(A kennings poem)

Hideous hag
Metallic monster
Electric-blue
Loud shrieker
Sea-dweller
Foe-finder
Blood-drawer
Killing claws.

Connie Leonard-Wright (9)
Preston Candover Primary School, Preston Candover

Grendel

(A kennings poem)

Murderous fiend
Killer of the night
Death-dealer
Mournful monster
Town trooper
Vicious claws
Scarred scales.

Josh Nash (10)
Preston Candover Primary School, Preston Candover

Grendel

(A kennings poem)

Creepy claws
Terrifying tail
Scary jaws
Blood nail
Soul sucker
Mad murderer
Writhing reptile.

Joshua Daniels (10)

Preston Candover Primary School, Preston Candover

Grendel's Mother

(A kennings poem)

Drool-dripper
Blood-drawer
Bone-breaker
Hideous hair
Killing claws
Ocean-haunter
Life-killer.

Jessamy Liney (8)
Preston Candover Primary School, Preston Candover

Grendel
(A kennings poem)

Scaly skin
Blood-dripping claws
Bone-snapping tail
Heart-ripper
Hideous hag
Chest-cruncher.

Jack Chapman (9)
Preston Candover Primary School, Preston Candover

Beowulf's Shield

(A kennings poem)

Never-breaker
Sword-deflector
Bullet-crusher
Spear-bruiser
Far-thrower
War-needler.

Maxim De Jersey Lowney (10)

Preston Candover Primary School, Preston Candover

Grendel's Mother

(A kennings poem)

Death-dealer
Razor-angry
Underwater ogress
Evil bone-breaker
Fatal daggers.

Sonny Freeman (8)

Preston Candover Primary School, Preston Candover

Sword
(A kennings poem)

Bone-breaker
Razor-sharp
Diamond-cracker
Heart-piercer
Shiny moonlight.

Roksana Sabina Owerczuk (9)
Preston Candover Primary School, Preston Candover

Grendel
(A kennings poem)

Heart-heaver
Bone-breaker
Heart-piercer
Earth-shaker
Blood-thirsty.

George Lang-Horgan (8)
Preston Candover Primary School, Preston Candover

Grendel

(A kennings poem)

Bone-breaker
Fear-bringer
Life-killer
Death-dealer
Tail-whipper.

Charlotte Sinclair (9)

Preston Candover Primary School, Preston Candover

YOUNG WRITERS INFORMATION

We hope you have enjoyed reading this book – and that you will continue to in the coming years.

If you're a young writer who enjoys reading and creative writing, or the parent of an enthusiastic poet or story writer, do visit our website **www.youngwriters.co.uk**. Here you will find free competitions, workshops and games, as well as recommended reads, a poetry glossary and our blog.

If you would like to order further copies of this book, or any of our other titles, then please give us a call or visit **www.youngwriters.co.uk**.

Young Writers
Remus House
Coltsfoot Drive
Peterborough
PE2 9BF
(01733) 890066
info@youngwriters.co.uk